Fresh Oil From Heaven

Fresh Oil From Heaven

Rodney M. Howard-Browne

RHBEA Publications

P.O. Box 197161, Louisville, KY 40259-7161 U.S.A.

P.O. Box 3900, Randburg 2125 South Africa

Unless otherwise indicated, all scriptural references are from the *King James Version* of the Bible.

Fresh Oil From Heaven
ISBN 0-9583066-2-1
Copyright 1992 by Rodney M. Howard-Browne

Published by RHBEA Publications
P.O. Box 197161, Louisville, KY 40259-7161 U.S.A.
P.O. Box 3900, Randburg 2125 South Africa

Printed in the United States of America

Fresh Oil From Heaven

Chapter 1
Fresh Oil or Stale?

In this book I would like to discuss a subject that is important to every believer especially in the day and age in which we are living. I remember conducting a revival in a church when the pastor asked me if I would minister to the sick by the laying on of hands and anoint them with oil.

I told him I would do it gladly and then I asked one of the ushers to bring me the "anointing oil." He did, but before I even saw the bottle of oil I smelt it — it stank. It was stale, rancid oil. I then sent the usher to get me some fresh oil — "three-in-one" Holy Ghost oil — down at the convenient store. I could not understand why people would want to use rancid, stale oil.

The Lord then spoke to me and said that was how many of His children smelled in the spirit. They stank from the stale oil of yesterday. In other words, that which they have is old and stale. The Lord desires His people to have something that is real, fresh, and vibrant.

God's plan for His people is to be anointed with fresh oil. Many Christians are living on yesterday's revelation, yesterday's bread. "I remember how it was back in 1919," they say. "I remember how it was when I was growing up." "If only we could go back to yesteryear." "If only it was back during the healing revival." "If only it were during the days of Brother Wigglesworth." "If only we could have walked in the days of Jesus and the Apostles." Yet, my Bible says that the prophets of old would have given anything to have been living in these days and times.

A Church That's Ready

You and I are living at the closing of the ages. We live at the most important time in human history. These exciting days are not the time to quit, not the time to throw up our hands in defeat. This is a time to work! The Bible says we must work while it is still day because the night is coming when no man can work. Jesus is coming soon! He wants a Church that's ready, that's prepared. If we are going to reach the world we need to be filled with the Holy Ghost — filled with fresh oil.

It's the same as with a new automobile. When you first purchase it, you have it serviced regularly and it's oil changed often so that it will last longer. If you would take so much care of something that is temporal, how much more should you take care of your heart and allow yourself to be serviced regularly by the Holy Spirit with fresh oil so that your Christian life might be sustained by the excitement of serving

2

God. So many of God's people, instead of maintaining themselves, allow themselves to be bound by a religious spirit which robs them of their joy. No wonder some people backslide or grow cold in their Christian walk.

One of the symbols of the Holy Spirit is oil. When you get oil, you will stop squeaking. The Church has too many squeaky Christians — always complaining, always squeaking. If the service is too long — squeak! If they don't like the preacher — squeeeak! If the worship service is long — squeak! When the Holy Ghost oil comes, it will get rid of all the squeaks and you will run smoothly.

> Wherefore I will yet plead with you, saith the Lord, and with your children's children will I plead.
>
> For pass over the isles of Chittim, and see; and send unto Kedar, and consider diligently, and see if there be such a thing.
>
> Hath a nation changed their gods, which are yet no gods? but my people have changed their glory for that which doth not profit.
>
> Be astonished, O ye heavens, at this, and be horribly afraid, be ye very desolate, saith the Lord.
>
> For my people have committed two evils; they have forsaken me the fountain of living waters, and hewed them out cisterns, broken cisterns, that can hold no water.
>
> **Jeremiah 2:9-13**

The Holy Spirit is also symbolized by water. Water brings refreshing to dry and thirsty land. Unfortunately, the Church has allowed itself to be satisfied with the counterfeit instead of striving for what is real. In this verse 13, we see that the hewn out cisterns, broken cisterns, are nothing other than religion and tradition. Religion is man's vain attempt to reach God, while Christianity is reaching man through Jesus Christ.

Ho, every one that thirsteth, come ye to the waters, and he that hath no money; come ye, buy, and eat; yea, come, buy wine and milk without money and without price.

Wherefore do ye spend money for that which is not bread? and your labour for that which satisfieth not?

Isaiah 55:1-2

What satisfies you?

So many people are trying to be satisfied and they find no satisfaction because the only thing that will satisfy is the Holy Spirit. He puts back into us what man lost. Adam had fellowship with God in the cool of the day but man lost that ability because sin came. Sin will separate you from God. The Holy Spirit has brought back the communion. If you, as a child of God, don't commune with the Holy Spirit, you are going to be dissatisfied. You can even come to church and yet be empty.

The Lord told me that certain places have much Word, but there is a famine in the land. The Word is like the sun. If the sun shines all the time and there is no rain, it will bring a drought. The Word has been shining and shining and shining, but there has been no rain of the Spirit of God, and it has brought a drought.

When the rain comes, there comes a flood, and it erodes everything. We have had the Word, the Word, the Word — but we need to have the Spirit. The sun and the rain together bring forth life.

Chapter 2
The Coming of the Bridegroom

Are You Wise or Foolish?

But of that day and hour knoweth no man, no, not the angels of heaven, but my Father only.

But as the days of Noe were, so shall also the coming of the Son of man be.

For as in the days that were before the flood they were eating and drinking, marrying and giving in marriage, until the day that Noe entered into the ark,

And knew not until the flood came, and took them all away; so shall also the coming of the Son of man be.

Then shall two be in the field; the one shall be taken, and the other left.

Two women shall be grinding at the mill; the one shall be taken, and the other left.

Watch therefore: for ye know not what hour your Lord doth come.

But know this, that if the goodman of the house had known in what watch the thief would come, he would have watched, and would not have suffered his house to be broken up.

Therefore be ye also ready . . .

Matthew 24:36-44

The Bible says in the last days there will be those who will say, "Where is the sign of His coming?" Let me tell you, He is coming! He wants you to be ready and the only way you are going to be ready is if you are full of the Holy Ghost — full of the oil!

Who then is a faithful and wise servant, whom his lord hath made ruler over his household, to give them meat in due season?

Blessed is that servant, whom his lord when he cometh shall find so doing.

Verily I say unto you, That he shall make him ruler over all his goods.

Matthew 24:45-47

You should live as if Jesus were coming today. Be ready — yet not expect Him for a hundred years. There are too many people saying things like, "We can't send our children to college because Jesus is coming." "We can't get married now because Jesus is coming." "We can't buy this house now because Jesus is coming." No, you should continue on and go about your daily life, planning ahead, but being ready, because He could come any moment. Are you ready to die right now?

If you are not ready, you had better get ready. We must stay ready at all times. Be ready to preach, ready to pray, ready to give a testimony — and ready to die at any moment.

> But and if that evil servant shall say in his heart, My lord delayeth his coming;
>
> And shall begin to smite his fellow servants, and to eat and drink with the drunken;
>
> The lord of that servant shall come in a day when he looketh not for him, and in an hour that he is not aware of,
>
> And shall cut him asunder, and appoint him his portion with the hypocrites: there shall be weeping and gnashing of teeth.
>
> Matthew 24:48-51

This is exactly what is happening to many in the Church right now. They are saying, "My Lord is delaying His coming." So they are smiting one another and eating and drinking with the world.

> Then shall the kingdom of heaven be likened unto ten virgins, which took their lamps, and went forth to meet the bridegroom.
>
> And five of them were wise, and five were foolish.

They that were foolish took their lamps, and took no oil with them:

But the wise took oil in their vessels with their lamps.

While the bridegroom tarried, they all slumbered and slept.

And at midnight there was a cry made, Behold, the bridegroom cometh: go ye out to meet him.

Matthew 25:1-6

I am telling you, there is a cry in the spirit that says, "Behold, the bridegroom cometh. Behold, the bridegroom cometh. Behold, the bridegroom cometh." He is coming! He is coming! It does not matter what you think. It does not matter what you believe or what your theology is. He is coming! He is not waiting for you to make up your mind and say, "Okay, Lord, You can come now." He is coming!

Then all those virgins arose, and trimmed their lamps.

And the foolish said unto the wise, Give us of your oil; for our lamps are gone out.

But the wise answered, saying, Not so; lest there be not enough for us and you: but go ye rather to them that sell, and buy for yourselves.

And while they went to buy, the bridegroom came; and they that were ready went in with him to the marriage: and the door was shut.

Afterward came also the other virgins, saying, Lord, Lord, open to us.

But he answered and said, Verily I say unto you, I know you not.

Watch therefore, for ye know neither the day nor the hour wherein the Son of man cometh.

Matthew 25:7-13

Do you want to be caught with your lamp empty? If you are not going for God, you are going against Him. If you are cold in your life and can't read your Bible, or you can't pray and you can't worship God, then there is something wrong. You need the oil of the Holy Ghost to come into your life.

Chapter 3
Prepare Your Hearts

The time has come to get ready. God is speaking to the Church. The time of preparation is here. The time has come to lay aside every weight and every sin that so easily besets us. The time has come to prepare our hearts, to prepare the inner man — not our heads — our spirits.

Wherefore seeing we also are compassed about with so great a cloud of witnesses, let us lay aside every weight, and the sin which doth so easily beset us, and let us run with patience the race that is set before us,

Looking unto Jesus the author and finisher of our faith; who for the joy that was set before him endured the cross, despising the shame, and is set down at the right hand of the throne of God.

For consider him that endured such contradiction of sinners against himself, lest ye be wearied and faint in your minds.

Ye have not yet resisted unto blood, striving against sin.

And ye have forgotten the exhortation which speaketh unto you as unto children, My son, despise not thou the chastening

13

of the Lord, nor faint when thou art rebuked of him:

For whom the Lord loveth he chasteneth, and scourgeth every son whom he receiveth.

If ye endure chastening, God dealeth with you as with sons; for what son is he whom the father chasteneth not?

But if ye be without chastisement, whereof all are partakers, then are ye bastards, and not sons.

Furthermore we have had fathers of our flesh which corrected us, and we gave them reverence: shall we not much rather be in subjection unto the Father of spirits, and live?

For they verily for a few days chastened us after their own pleasure; but he for our profit, that we might be partakers of his holiness.

Now no chastening for the present seemeth to be joyous, but grievous: nevertheless afterward it yieldeth the peaceable fruit of righteousness unto them which are exercised thereby.

Wherefore lift up the hands which hang down, and the feeble knees;

And make straight paths for your feet, lest that which is lame be turned out of the way; but let it rather be healed.

Follow peace with all men, and holiness, without which no man shall see the Lord:

Looking diligently lest any man fail of the grace of God; lest any root of bitterness springing up trouble you, and thereby many be defiled;

Lest there be any fornicator, or profane person, as Esau, who for one morsel of meat sold his birthright.

For ye know how that afterward, when he would have inherited the blessing, he was rejected: for he found no place of repentance, though he sought it carefully with tears.

For ye are not come unto the mount that might be touched, and that burned with fire, nor unto blackness, and darkness, and tempest,

And the sound of a trumpet, and the voice of words; which voice they that heard intreated that the word should not be spoken to them any more:

(For they could not endure that which was commanded, And if so much as a beast touch the mountain, it shall be stoned, or thrust through with a dart:

And so terrible was the sight, that Moses said, I exceedingly fear and quake:)

But ye are come unto mount Sion, and unto the city of the living God, the heavenly Jerusalem, and to an innumerable company of angels,

To the general assembly and church of the firstborn, which are written in heaven, and to

God the Judge of all, and to the spirits of just men made perfect,

And to Jesus the mediator of the new covenant, and to the blood of sprinkling, that speaketh better things than that of Abel.

See that ye refuse not him that speaketh. For if they escaped not who refused him that spake on earth, much more shall not we escape, if we turn away from him that speaketh from heaven:

Whose voice then shook the earth: but now he hath promised, saying, Yet once more I shake not the earth only, but also heaven.

And this word, Yet once more, signifieth the removing of those things that are shaken, as of things that are made, that those things which cannot be shaken may remain.

Wherefore we receiving a kingdom which cannot be moved, let us have grace, whereby we may serve God acceptably with reverence and godly fear:

For our God is a consuming fire.

Hebrews 12:1-29

It is time for God's people to have a breakthrough in the spirit. It is time for a breakthrough in their soul, a breakthrough in their body.

The devil has kept the Church in bondage long enough. When you get the oil of the Holy Ghost, it will come on you like a mighty fire. God will light a match of the fire of the Holy

16

Ghost and will set you aflame, and you will march through the land like a mighty firebrand, blazing the trail of the Holy Ghost.

If you will open your heart to the Lord Jesus Christ and hearken to the Spirit of God, He will send a flame forth right from where you are. It will burn through your city and your state; it will go into the foothills and plains; it will burn through the highways and byways. Revival will spread like a mighty fire and the glory of God will be sent!

This is the day of the outpouring of the fresh oil of the Holy Ghost. It is for you and for whosoever will — let them come and drink of the fountain of living water!

Revival begins in you!

Revival must begin in you. It cannot begin in your neighbor for you. Forget about everyone else. Concentrate on yourself. Where do you stand with God? How full is your lamp? How trimmed is your lamp? How ready are you? Forget about neighbors and family members — what about you?

Wherefore (as the Holy Ghost saith, To day if ye will hear his voice,

Harden not your hearts, as in the provocation, in the day of temptation in the wilderness:

When your fathers tempted me, proved me, and saw my works forty years.

Wherefore I was grieved with that generation, and said, They do always err in their heart; and they have not known my ways.

So I sware in my wrath, They shall not enter into my rest.)

Take heed, brethren, lest there be in any of you an evil heart of unbelief, in departing from the living God.

But exhort one another daily, while it is called To day; lest any of you be hardened through the deceitfulness of sin.

Hebrews 3:7-13

One of the problems in the Church is that it is hardened with the deceitfulness of sin. Daily we are to exhort one another. Don't ever say that you can make it without your brothers and sisters. Don't ever say you don't need to go to church. "We have tapes; we can listen to tapes," you say. "It is the only time we have to spend with the family."

The Bible says forsake not the gathering of yourselves together, the more so as you see the Day approaching (Hebrews 10:25.) The Day is approaching! We are closer today than we have ever been. There is an urgency in my spirit. The clock is ticking away and there is a job to be done.

For we are made partakers of Christ, if we hold the beginning of our confidence stedfast unto the end;

While it is said, To day if ye will hear his voice, harden not your hearts, as in the provocation.

For some, when they had heard, did provoke: howbeit not all that came out of Egypt by Moses.

But with whom was he grieved forty years? was it not with them that had sinned, whose carcases fell in the wilderness?

And to whom sware he that they should not enter into his rest, but to them that believed not?

So we see that they could not enter in because of unbelief.

Hebrews 3:14-19

You will not move in the Holy Ghost if you allow your heart to be hardened and if you allow it to be embalmed with unbelief.

Some Christians believe nothing God is doing. If someone is raised from the dead, they ask, "How do you know he was dead?" If God blew the roof off they would say it wasn't bolted down properly. They are always skeptical, always full of doubt, always full of unbelief. We have to change! What is it that causes us to have unbelief? It is the deceitfulness of sin.

For the time is come that judgement must begin at the house of God.

First Peter 4:17

Oh, people don't want to hear that! They want to stay with the "nice" Scriptures. They attach all their faith to Philippians 4:19 and similar passages. Yet, this is just as much the Bible as Philippians 4:19 is — and the Bible says all Scripture is profitable for reproof, correction, and instruction in righteousness, that the man of God may be perfect, thoroughly furnished unto all good works (Second Timothy 3:16). You must be thoroughly furnished. Let it be known to all men and to all the demons in hell that you are full of the oil of the Holy Ghost and that your lamp is trimmed.

The time has come that judgment must begin at the house of God. If it first begins at us, what shall the end be of them that obey not the gospel of God? Presently, the world is laughing. But they haven't seen God in His power and in His glory. They sit in their ivory towers and they mock the things of God and the move of God and the ministers of the gospel. The day is coming when God will say, "That's it — I've had enough." The power of God will sweep through the land. The glory of God will be seen. People will be mocking the Spirit of God and they will fall dead.

God is not mocked. God intends to purge the Church, to make it the vessel He wants. Then we will go forth in power and He will begin to judge the world. There will come some natural disaster too — whole cities will be swallowed up in earthquakes. The Bible says in the last days perilous times will come.

We are living on the brink of the greatest revival of the Holy Ghost. Every one of you can be a part of it. If you will clean up your act and say, "God, I am so tired of everything. I don't want anything else. I just want to live for You. I don't desire anything else. God do whatever You have to do in my life. Change me, fill me with Your oil. I want to be a part of that move. I want to be in the ranks. I want to be a part of the troops. I want to be part of that army. I don't want to be left at bootcamp. I want to be out in the front lines!"

If the righteous scarcely be saved, where shall the ungodly and the sinner appear?

Wherefore let them that suffer according to the will of God commit the keeping of their souls to him in well doing, as unto a faithful Creator.

1 Peter 4:18,19

God wants to do a work in your heart. He is not going to stroll along and do it while you sit there in your recliner rocker, watching television and sipping soda. As a commercial break comes you say, "Holy Ghost now is Your chance," and you expect Him to move. No, you have to separate yourself, get hungry, cry out for Him. You have to pray.

21

I know that I would rather die than not have the anointing. If God told me I couldn't walk in His anointing, then I would ask Him to take me home, because there would be nothing else to live for. God wants to make us vessels that He can flow through. But we must cry out to Him, "God, I desire to be used of You. Use me, Lord. Use me, O God. Use me!" Then He will come and He will use you.

Some people don't believe this. They think they can say, "God, You are looking for some-body with all these qualifications. Well, I have this degree and this diploma. You really can't do without me. If You don't take me, Your king-dom will suffer. God, if You don't have me, You know the world will suffer. I'm indispensable!"

Yes, God wants you. But God can do without you. Don't ever think that without you, heaven will close down. Without you, God will quit and resign, and leave the throne. He already left heaven once, when He came here to die for mankind, and rose again.

There must be a hunger. The Word says, "The effectual fervent prayer of a righteous man availeth much" (James 5:16). There is a story about a certain man, who would lie face down in the snow and pray. The snow for meters around him would melt because of the fervor of his pray-ing.

People don't want to do that today. They will "pray" in a room where the television is on, so that they can watch the ball game while they are praying. Call a church barbecue and watch them come by the hundreds — but call a prayer meeting, perhaps an all night prayer meeting, and listen to the excuses. "I'm so tired, pastor. I've been working all week."

You must want the Holy Ghost. You must thirst for Him. You must desire the anointing more than anything else in life. You must want it more than you want life itself. You have to mean business with God, get serious with God. It is just not a quick stroll down the aisle to have a hand slapped on your head. You have to desire it, intensely desire it from the bottom of your heart and from the core of your being. You cry out to God, "Do whatever You have to do, but please, let me be a part of it. Do a work in my heart!" God can do a work in your heart.

God will work on some people like He did on Saul. The Lord knocked him clean off his horse and made him blind for three days and nights. Some people who totally oppose God will be dealt with like that. I have never had something like that come my way, neither have the majority of us. Generally, it is those who have desired it and called out for it.

Read the life stories of some of the great men of God, men like A. A. Allen. He locked himself in a room, and told his wife not to let him out, even if he screamed. When he eventually walked out of that room, the glory of God was all over him. He was anointed with fresh oil!

Everybody wants a ministry, but nobody wants to pay the price to become the vessel God wants.

Chapter 4
My Testimony — When God First Anointed Me

I was born and raised in a Pentecostal home. As I grew up I frequently saw supernatural occurances and miracles. On one occasion, my mother broke her arm in three places. One of the breaks was so bad that it broke her watch strap and the bone stood up higher than her wrist. Our pastor came and laid hands on her and the power of God went through her arm like electricity and she knew she was healed.

I must have been about six years old, and when she said she was going to cut the plaster cast off because she was healed, I pleaded with her not to. To me, if something was broken, it was broken. If she took off the cast, I thought her arm would fall off! She cut the cast off, praying in the Holy Ghost, and came out of the room with her arm raised — totally healed — only four days after it had been broken!

My parents would sometimes pray from seven in the evening until two in the morning. People would come to the house and not want to leave because the presence of God was there, the anointing of God was there. Demon-possessed

25

people would come into the house and start to scream because the glory of God was in the house!

We would sit at the table and my father would start to pray. I could tell from the way he prayed whether we were about to eat or whether we would eat hours later as the anointing of God would come upon him and he would begin to prophesy. My mother would put the food back into the oven. She knew we were about to have church!

Yet, I knew there was more! In 1979, I cried out to God for it. I wanted Him to manifest Himself to me and in me. I was hungry. He told me you have to hunger and thirst, and at first I said to Him, "Why don't You just give it to me? I have served You all my life. I have been a good boy. I haven't done this, I haven't done that, like others have. God, I deserve it."

He said, "I'm not a respecter of persons. You come the same way everyone else does. You come in faith and you get hungry and you desire it, and then I'll give it to you."

We have to desire the anointing oil like a man who has been in the desert for three days desires water. All he can cry for is water. If a man walks up to him and offers him half a million dollars, he will push him aside and shout, "No! Water, water, WATER!" He wants water more than life itself, because the only thing that is going to save him is water.

When you become desperate for the Holy Ghost in your life like that, so that you want nothing else, then He will come. There is something about a thirsty and hungry heart that will cause God's power to move over a million people to come to your house.

It depends on you. How hungry are you? How desperate are you for fresh oil?

I must have called out to God for about twenty minutes that day. The fire of God came on me. It started on my head and went right down to my feet. His power burned in my body and stayed like that for four days. I thought I was going to die. I thought He was going to kill me. I was plugged into heaven's electric light supply and since then, my desire has been to go and plug other people in.

My whole body was on fire from the top of my head to the soles of my feet and out of my belly began to flow a river of living water. I began to laugh uncontrollably and then I began to weep and then speak with other tongues.

This continued not for one hour only, but for hours on end. I was so intoxicated on the wine of the Holy Ghost that I was beside myself. The fire of God was coursing through my whole being and it didn't quit. One day, two days, three days, and in the fourth day I couldn't bear it anymore.

I began to realize why we would need a glorified body when we get to heaven. When the natural comes into contact with the supernatural, some thing has to give way and it's not going to be the supernatural.

I began to think, *The Lord has heard my prayer. He heard me say, "Either You come down here and touch me or I am going to come up there and touch You,"* and now He's come to touch me and He's going to take me home. I began to beg Him to lift the anointing off me so that I could bear it. He did, and I was aware of it staying lightly on me for another two weeks. Because of this encounter with the Lord, my life was radically changed from that day on.

I am so tired of those meetings where they tell you about the things of God, but they never tell you how to get it. The Lord told me to teach on the anointing, and the fire of God has been falling since I started doing that. He said, "Give me an opportunity to move and I will move." He told me to lay hands on people and get them saturated with the Holy Ghost. I was not to take my hands off until they are drunk in the Holy Ghost. So He connects them, plugs them into heaven's light socket.

When people lie under the power, they are on God's operating table. Leave them alone there! Don't interfere with them. God is busy with them. When hands are laid on you, don't look to man, look to God. He will meet with you and your life will be changed. He will burn things out of you, things that are holding you back, things that are oppressing you, things that keep you in fear and bondage.

The Lord said there are so many of His people bound with the cares of this life, strife, unforgiveness, and bitterness. You can't receive blessing until you get rid of that stuff. So let the fire of the Holy Ghost fall and burn it out of you and fill you up with fresh oil. Then the world will look at you and acknowledge the fact that though you may be unlearned and ignorant, you have been with Jesus.

When you spend time in the presence of God, you become saturated and permeated with the anointing of God. You will go and touch people and the glory of God will go into them.

The day is coming when people will go into supermarkets and places of business and there they will fall under the power of God. His glory will be seen on the streets!

He wants to anoint you with fresh oil. If you are a backslider, He wants to anoint you with fresh oil. It doesn't matter what you have done. He wants to touch your life and give you a miracle.

Don't hold back. Go to God and cry out to Him to touch you — He will anoint you when you desire Him to. It is up to you!

The words of this wonderful song should be the cry of our hearts.

> Lord, anoint us with fresh oil
> The anointing upon us renew
> That we may cease to be weary
> And go forth with our strength renewed.

Sermon Outline:
Fresh Oil From Heaven

Foundation Scriptures — Psalm 92:1-15 and Jeremiah 2:9-13.

1. *Some people have run dry —fresh or stale oil?*
   a. Live in the past — 1948.
   b. Jeremiah 2:9-13.
   c. Isaiah 55:1-2.

2. *Are you wise or foolish?*
   a. Matthew 24:26-51
   b. Matthew 25:1-13
   c. Five wise and five foolish
   d. i. They were all virgins
      ii. They were all waiting for the Bridegroom
      iii. They all had lamps
      iv. Five were wise and took oil in reserve
      v. Five were foolish — did not have enough to last them through the night
   e. Do you have enough — are you wise or foolish?
   f. Make ready for the Bridegroom

3. *Prepare your hearts*
   a. Hebrews 12:1-29
   b. Hebrews 3:7-19
   c. 1 Peter 4:17,18

31

4. *My Testimony: When God first anointed me.*

   How to be anointed with fresh oil from heaven.
   a. Hunger for it
   b. Receive it and drink
   c. Ephesians 5:18-21

For information regarding books, audio tapes, and videotapes, please write us at Rodney Howard-Browne Evangelistic Association at one of the addresses listed below:

RHBEA Publications

P.O. Box 197161, Louisville, KY 40259-7161 U.S.A.
P.O. Box 3900, Randburg 2125 South Africa